Functional Programming with Python:

A Practical Manual for Developing Clean, Reliable
Applications, Harnessing Parallelism, Simplifying
Testing, and Creating Durable Code."

Matthew D.Passmore

Table of Content

11.2 Showcasing Benefits of Functional Techniques in Different Scenarios

Part 1: Foundations of Functional Programming

Chapter 1

Introduction to Functional Programming

Functional programming is a programming paradigm that emphasizes functions as the building blocks of applications. It focuses on concepts like immutability, pure functions, and avoiding side effects to build clean, reliable, and easier-to-reason-about software.

Here's a breakdown of the core ideas:

Functions as First-Class Citizens: In functional programming, functions are treated just like any other data type. You can assign them to variables, pass them as arguments to other functions, and even return them from functions. This allows for creating powerful abstractions and composable code.

Immutability: Functional programming encourages using immutable data structures. This means that once a data structure is created, its value cannot be modified. Instead, you create a new data structure with the desired changes. This simplifies reasoning about program state and avoids unexpected side effects.

Pure Functions: Pure functions are functions that always return the same output for a given set of inputs, and don't produce any side effects (like modifying global state or external resources). This makes them predictable, easier to test, and suitable for parallel execution.

Here are some of the benefits of using functional programming:

Improved Code Clarity and Maintainability: By breaking down problems into smaller, well-defined functions, functional code tends to be more readable and easier to understand.

Enhanced Testability: Pure functions with no side effects are easier to test and reason about, as their behavior is always predictable for a given input.

Potential for Better Parallelization: The absence of side effects in functional programs makes them suitable for parallel execution on multiple cores or processors, potentially improving performance.

Overall, functional programming offers a different way of thinking about problem-solving in software development. By embracing its core principles, you can create more robust, reliable, and easier-to-maintain applications.

1.1 What is Functional Programming?

Functional programming is a programming paradigm that emphasizes functions as the building blocks of applications. It focuses on concepts like immutability, pure functions, and avoiding side effects to build clean, reliable, and easier-to-reason-about software.

Here's a breakdown of the core ideas:

Functions as First-Class Citizens: In functional programming, functions are treated just like any other data type. You can assign them to variables, pass them as arguments to other functions, and even return them from functions. This allows for creating powerful abstractions and composable code.

Immutability: Functional programming encourages using immutable data structures. This means that once a data structure is created, its value cannot be modified. Instead, you create a new data structure with the desired changes. This simplifies reasoning about program state and avoids unexpected side effects.

Pure Functions: Pure functions are functions that always return the same output for a given set of inputs, and don't produce any side effects (like modifying global state or external resources). This makes them predictable, easier to test, and suitable for parallel execution.

Here are some of the benefits of using functional programming:

Improved Code Clarity and Maintainability: By breaking down problems into smaller, well-defined functions, functional code tends to be more readable and easier to understand.

Enhanced Testability: Pure functions with no side effects are easier to test and reason about, as their behavior is always predictable for a given input.

Potential for Better Parallelization: The absence of side effects in functional programs makes them suitable for parallel execution on multiple cores or processors, potentially improving performance.

Overall, functional programming offers a different way of thinking about problem-solving in software development. By embracing its core principles, you can create more robust, reliable, and easier-to-maintain applications.

1.2 Benefits of Functional Programming

Functional programming offers a distinct set of advantages that can significantly improve the quality and maintainability of your code. Here are some of the key benefits:

Improved Code Clarity and Maintainability: Functional programming emphasizes breaking down problems into smaller, well-defined functions. This modular approach leads to code that is easier to read, understand, and reason about. Complex logic can be decomposed into smaller, reusable functions, making the codebase more manageable.

Enhanced Testability: A core principle of functional programming is pure functions. Pure functions always return the same output for a given set of inputs, and avoid side effects. This predictability makes functional code significantly easier to test. You can isolate individual functions and verify their behavior with confidence, leading to more robust and reliable applications.

Potential for Better Parallelization: The absence of side effects in functional programs makes them well-suited for parallel execution on multiple cores or processors. Since there's no risk of one function unexpectedly modifying data relied upon by another, functional programs can be efficiently divided and run concurrently, potentially leading to performance improvements.

Reduced Bugs: Immutability, a core concept in functional programming, encourages you to create new data structures with the desired changes rather than modifying existing ones. This helps to avoid unintended side effects and mutations that can introduce bugs into your codebase.

Simpler Debugging: Functional code tends to be more modular and have fewer dependencies due to its focus on pure functions. This simplifies debugging as you can isolate issues more easily by focusing on specific functions and their inputs and outputs.

Concurrency Made Easier: Reasoning about thread safety is a common challenge in concurrent programming. Functional programming's emphasis on immutability and pure functions naturally avoids many common concurrency issues, making it easier to develop safe and reliable concurrent applications.

Overall, functional programming offers a paradigm shift that can lead to cleaner, more reliable, and easier-to-maintain code. By leveraging its principles, you can develop robust applications that are well-suited for the multi-core processors prevalent in modern computing.

1.3 Core Concepts of Functional Programming.

.

Functional programming relies on a foundation of core concepts that differentiate it from other programming paradigms like object-oriented programming. Here's a breakdown of some of the essential ideas:

Functions as First-Class Citizens: In functional programming, functions are treated just like any other data type, such as integers or strings. This means you can:

Assign them to variables

Pass them as arguments to other functions

Return them from functions

This ability to treat functions as values empowers you to create powerful abstractions and build highly composable code. Complex problems can be tackled by composing smaller, reusable functions.

Immutability: Functional programming encourages the use of immutable data structures. This means that once a data structure is created, its value cannot be modified. Instead, when you need to make changes, you create a new data structure with the desired modifications.

This focus on immutability has several advantages:

Simplifies reasoning about program state: Since data isn't unexpectedly changing, it's easier to track and predict how the program behaves.

Reduces bugs caused by side effects: Mutations can lead to unintended consequences and errors. Immutability helps to avoid these issues.

Pure Functions: Pure functions are functions that consistently return the same output for a given set of inputs, and without producing any side effects. They don't modify global state or external resources. This characteristic makes them:

Predictable: Their behavior is always clear for a given input, simplifying reasoning about the code.

Easier to test: The consistent output for known inputs makes them more testable and reliable.

Suitable for parallelization: The lack of side effects allows pure functions to be safely run concurrently on multiple processors potentially improving performance.

By embracing these core concepts, functional programming fosters a style of development that prioritizes clean, modular, and reliable code.

Chapter 2.

Functions as First-Class Citizens

In functional programming, functions are treated like superstars – they are not relegated to the background, but instead are considered "first-class citizens" just like any other data type (like numbers or strings). This means you can treat functions in powerful ways that make your code more flexible and reusable. Here's what it entails:

1. Assigning Functions to Variables:

Imagine having a special box that can hold not just numbers or text, but also instructions on how to do something. In functional programming, variables can store functions like these boxes. You can assign a function to a variable, giving it a name for easy reference later. For instance:

Python
```
def greet(name):
  """Greets the person by name."""
  return f"Hello, {name}!"
```

```python
# Assign the greet function to a variable say_hello
say_hello = greet

# Now you can use the variable to call the function
result = say_hello("Alice")
print(result)  # Output: Hello, Alice!
```
Use code with caution.

content_copy

2. Passing Functions as Arguments:

Functions can be incredibly helpful to other functions. Just like you can pass data (like numbers or strings) as arguments to functions, you can also pass functions as arguments! This allows you to create functions that operate on other functions, making your code more modular and flexible.

Here's an example:

Python
```python
def compose_greeting(func, name):
```

```python
    """Composes a greeting using the provided
function."""
  return func(name)

# Pass the greet function as an argument to
compose_greeting
composed_message = compose_greeting(greet, "Bob")
print(composed_message) # Output: Hello, Bob!
```
Use code with caution.
content_copy

3. Returning Functions from Functions:

Not only can functions accept functions as arguments, but they can also return functions! This creates a powerful capability for building functions that generate other functions. Imagine a function that's like a function factory, able to produce specialized functions based on certain criteria.

Here's a simplified example:

Python
```python
def create_greeter(greeting):
```

```python
    """Creates a function that returns a greeting with the
provided message."""
    def greet(name):
        return f"{greeting}, {name}!"
    return greet


# Call create_greeter to get a new function
morning_greeter = create_greeter("Good morning")


# Use the returned function to generate greetings
morning_message = morning_greeter("Charlie")
print(morning_message)    # Output: Good morning,
Charlie!
```
Use code with caution.

content_copy

By treating functions as first-class citizens, functional
programming empowers you to write code that is more
expressive, reusable, and easier to reason about. It
allows you to create functions that operate on other
functions, leading to more modular and powerful
programs.

2.1 Defining and Working with Functions in Python

.

In Python, functions are fundamental building blocks that allow you to organize your code, promote reusability, and improve readability. Here's a breakdown of how to define and work with functions effectively:

Defining Functions:

The def keyword: You use the def keyword to mark the beginning of a function definition. It's followed by the function's name and parentheses.

Parameters: Inside the parentheses, you can specify parameters (arguments) that the function will accept. These parameters act like placeholders for values that will be provided when the function is called. Parameters are optional; if a function doesn't require any input, you can leave the parentheses empty.

Docstring (Optional): A docstring is a concise explanation of what the function does and how to use it. It's added as a string right after the function definition, enclosed in triple quotation marks (""" or '"). While not mandatory, docstrings are highly recommended for improving code clarity and maintainability.

Function Body: The indented block of code below the function definition lines represents the function's body. This is where you write the statements that the function will execute when called.

Return Statement (Optional): A function can optionally return a value using the return statement. The return statement specifies the value the function will send back to the caller after its execution. If no return statement is included, the function implicitly returns None.

Here's an example of a function that greets someone by name:

```python
Python
def greet(name):
    """Greets the person by name and returns the greeting."""
    return f"Hello, {name}!"
```

```
# Call the greet function with an argument
message = greet("Alice")
print(message)  # Output: Hello, Alice!
Use code with caution.
content_copy
```

Working with Functions:

Calling Functions: To execute a function, you use its name followed by parentheses. Inside the parentheses, you can provide the required arguments (values) separated by commas, matching the order and number of parameters defined in the function.

Arguments vs. Parameters: Remember that parameters are placeholders within the function definition, while arguments are the actual values you provide when calling the function.

Assigning Return Values: When a function returns a value, you can assign that value to a variable to capture the output. This allows you to use the function's result in other parts of your code.

Key Points:

Functions promote code reusability. By defining a function once, you can call it multiple times with different arguments to achieve similar tasks.
Functions improve code readability and organization. Breaking down complex logic into smaller, well-defined functions makes code easier to understand and maintain.

In conclusion, effectively defining and working with functions is essential for writing clean, maintainable, and reusable Python code.

2.2 Higher-Order Functions

.

Higher-order functions are a cornerstone of functional programming and add a new level of power and flexibility to your Python code. They are functions that:

Accept Other Functions as Arguments: Unlike regular functions that take data as input, higher-order functions can take other functions as arguments. This allows you to pass functionality around like any other value.

Return Functions as Outputs: Higher-order functions can also return functions as their output. This lets you create functions that generate or customize other functions based on specific criteria.

Here's how higher-order functions unlock new possibilities:

Abstraction and Reusability: By encapsulating logic within functions that can be passed around, higher-order functions promote code abstraction and reusability. You can create generic functions that operate on other functions, reducing redundancy and making your code more adaptable.

Functional Composition: Higher-order functions enable functional composition, a powerful technique for building complex logic by chaining smaller functions together. Each function performs a specific step, and the output of one function becomes the input for the next. This creates a readable and modular way to handle complex tasks.

Here are some common examples of higher-order functions in Python:

map(): Applies a function to all elements of an iterable (like a list or string) and returns a new iterable with the results.

filter(): Creates a new iterable with elements from the original iterable that pass a test defined by a function.

reduce(): Applies a function repeatedly to an iterable, reducing it to a single value. (Note: reduce is less commonly used in modern Python due to potential performance issues and the availability of other functional constructs.)

Example using map():

Python
```
def square(x):
  """Returns the square of a number."""
  return x * x


numbers = [1, 2, 3, 4]
squared_numbers = map(square, numbers) # Pass square function as argument to map

# map returns an iterator, convert it to a list for easy printing
print(list(squared_numbers)) # Output: [1, 4, 9, 16]
```
Use code with caution.

content_copy

By understanding and leveraging higher-order functions, you can write more concise, expressive, and composable Python code.

2.3 Lambda Expressions

Lambda expressions, also known as anonymous functions, are a concise way to define small, single-expression functions in Python. They are particularly useful in functional programming for creating functions on-the-fly within function calls or assignments.

Here's a breakdown of lambda expressions:

Syntax:

lambda arguments: expression
lambda: This keyword introduces the lambda expression.
arguments: (Optional) A comma-separated list of arguments the function can accept.
expression: The single expression that defines the function's body. This expression is evaluated and returned when the lambda function is called.
Key Points:

Single Expression: Lambda expressions are limited to a single expression. For more complex logic, you should use traditional function definitions.

Anonymous: Lambda functions don't have a name, hence the term "anonymous." They are defined and used inline within your code.

Often Used with Higher-Order Functions: Lambda expressions are frequently used in conjunction with higher-order functions like map, filter, and reduce to provide the logic for those functions to operate on.

Example using map() with a lambda expression:

Python
numbers = [1, 2, 3, 4]
squared_numbers = map(lambda x: x * x, numbers) #
Lambda function to square each number

print(list(squared_numbers)) # Output: [1, 4, 9, 16]
Use code with caution.
content_copy
In this example, the lambda expression lambda x: x * x squares each number in the numbers list when used with the map function.

Use Cases for Lambda Expressions:

Simple, Disposable Functions: When you need a small, one-time-use function, lambda expressions offer a concise way to define it without cluttering your code with named functions.

Sorting with Custom Criteria: You can use lambda expressions as key functions for sorting, allowing you to define custom sorting logic based on specific criteria within your sort operation.

Filtering with Conditions: When filtering elements based on specific conditions, lambda expressions can provide a clean way to define the filtering logic within the filter function call.

While lambda expressions provide a convenient way to define small functions, they are not always the best choice. If you need a more complex function with reusability or readability in mind, a traditional function definition is generally preferred.

Chapter 3.

Immutability and Pure Functions

Immutability and pure functions are fundamental concepts that go hand-in-hand in functional programming. They both contribute to writing clean, predictable, and easier-to-reason-about code.

Immutability:

In functional programming, immutability refers to the idea that once a data structure is created, its value cannot be modified. This means you cannot change the elements within a list, dictionary, or other data structure after its creation.

Instead, when you need to make changes, you create a new data structure with the desired modifications. The original data structure remains unchanged.

Benefits of Immutability:

Simpler Reasoning About Program State: Since data isn't unexpectedly changing throughout the program, it's easier to track and predict how the program behaves. This makes debugging easier and reduces the risk of errors caused by unintended side effects.

Improved Thread Safety: In multi-threaded environments, immutability eliminates the need for complex synchronization mechanisms to protect data from being modified by multiple threads simultaneously. This makes your code safer and more efficient when dealing with concurrency.

Functional Data Structures: Many functional programming languages provide built-in immutable data structures that enforce immutability by design. These structures offer efficient ways to create new versions of the data with modifications.

Pure Functions:

A pure function is a function that adheres to the following principles:

Deterministic: Given the same input, it always returns the same output.

No Side Effects: It doesn't produce any side effects, such as modifying global state or external resources (like files or network connections).

Referential Transparency: If a part of your code calls a pure function with a specific input, you can replace that call with the function's output without affecting the program's behavior.

Why Pure Functions Matter:

Predictable Behavior: Pure functions are predictable because they always produce the same output for a given set of inputs. This makes reasoning about them and testing them much easier.

Testability: The lack of side effects allows you to isolate pure functions and test them independently with confidence in the expected outcome for given inputs.

Parallelization: Since pure functions don't have side effects, they are well-suited for parallel execution on multiple cores or processors. There's no risk of one

function unexpectedly modifying data relied upon by another, enabling potential performance improvements.
The Immutability-Purity Connection:

Immutability and pure functions work together to create a powerful paradigm for functional programming.

By using immutable data structures, you naturally avoid side effects of modifying existing data. This promotes the creation of pure functions that rely on the inputs they receive and don't modify anything outside their scope.

Pure functions, in turn, benefit from the predictability and lack of side effects that immutability brings.
In essence, immutability and pure functions are essential building blocks for functional programming, leading to more reliable, maintainable, and easier-to-understand code.

3.1 The Power of Immutability

Immutability, a core principle in functional programming, offers a surprising amount of power when it comes to writing clean, reliable, and predictable code. Here's a deeper dive into why immutability is so advantageous:

Simplified Reasoning About Program State: When data structures are immutable, their state remains constant after creation. This eliminates the mental overhead of tracking potential modifications throughout your code. You can reason about the program's behavior with greater confidence, as the data you're working with won't unexpectedly change under the hood.

Reduced Bugs from Side Effects: Mutable data structures can lead to unintended side effects. Imagine a function that modifies a list you're using elsewhere in your code. This can cause unexpected behavior and bugs that are difficult to track down. Immutability eliminates this risk. When you need to make changes, you create a new data structure, leaving the original intact. This ensures that other parts of your code that rely on the original data are not affected by the modifications.

Enhanced Thread Safety: In multithreaded environments, where multiple threads can access and modify data simultaneously, immutability shines. Mutable data structures require complex synchronization mechanisms (like locks) to prevent race conditions where threads overwrite each other's changes. By using immutable data structures, you eliminate the need for these mechanisms altogether. Since each thread works with its own copy of the data, there's no risk of conflicts, simplifying concurrent programming and reducing the potential for thread-related errors.

Improved Testability: Pure functions, which are functions that rely on immutability, are significantly easier to test. Because they have no side effects and always return the same output for a given set of inputs, you can isolate them and test their behavior with confidence. This leads to more robust and reliable code.

Functional Data Structures: Many functional programming languages provide built-in immutable data structures like lists, sets, and maps. These structures offer efficient ways to create new versions of the data with the desired modifications. For instance, instead of modifying an existing list in place, you can create a new list with the updated elements, leaving the original list untouched. This promotes a functional style of programming where you focus on creating new data structures rather than mutating existing ones.

Declarative vs. Imperative Programming: Immutability encourages a declarative style of programming. You focus on what the desired outcome is, rather than how to achieve it through a series of mutations. This can lead to more concise and readable code, as the intent becomes clearer.

In conclusion, immutability is not just a quirk of functional programming; it's a powerful tool that can significantly improve the quality and maintainability of your code. By embracing immutability, you write code that is easier to reason about, less prone to bugs, and more suitable for concurrent programming and testing. It's a shift in mindset that can unlock a new level of clarity, reliability, and maintainability in your software development.

3.2 Designing Pure Functions

.Here's a breakdown on designing pure functions in functional programming:

Core Principles of Pure Functions:

Deterministic Output: A pure function always returns the same output for a given set of inputs. No matter how many times you call a pure function with the same arguments, you'll always get the same result. This predictability makes reasoning about program behavior much easier.

No Side Effects: Pure functions don't produce any side effects. This means they don't modify global state, external resources (like files or network connections), or have any observable effects outside of returning a value. They rely solely on the inputs they receive.

Referential Transparency: This principle states that if you replace a call to a pure function with its return value, the program's behavior remains unchanged. Since pure functions only depend on their inputs and have no side effects, their output can be treated as a replacement for the function call itself in certain contexts.

Benefits of Pure Functions:

Improved Testability: The predictable behavior of pure functions makes them significantly easier to test. You can isolate them and test their outputs for specific inputs with confidence, leading to more robust and reliable code.

Parallelization Potential: The absence of side effects allows pure functions to be safely executed in parallel on multiple cores or processors. There's no risk of one function interfering with another by modifying shared data, potentially improving performance.

Simpler Reasoning: Pure functions promote a declarative style of programming. You focus on what the function should output for a given input, rather than how to achieve it through a series of modifications. This leads to cleaner and more readable code.

Designing Pure Functions in Practice:

Avoid Global State and External Interactions: Don't modify global variables or access external resources like files or network connections within pure functions. These actions introduce external dependencies and make the function's behavior less predictable.

Use Immutable Data Structures: Whenever possible, use immutable data structures (like those specifically designed for functional programming languages) as inputs and outputs for your pure functions. This ensures that the function isn't modifying the original data and reinforces the concept of referential transparency.

Focus on Calculations and Transformations: Pure functions should primarily focus on performing calculations, transformations, or manipulations on the data they receive as input. Avoid incorporating actions that produce side effects.

Return New Data Structures: If a function needs to modify data, create a new data structure with the desired changes and return that new structure. This maintains immutability and ensures the original data remains untouched.

Examples of Pure vs. Impure Functions:

Pure:
Python
```python
def add(x, y):
    """Returns the sum of two numbers."""
    return x + y


result = add(5, 3)  # result will always be 8
```
Use code with caution.
content_copy
Impure (modifies global state):
Python
```python
global_count = 0
```

```python
def increment_count():
  """Increments a global variable (impure)."""
  global global_count
  global_count += 1

increment_count()
increment_count()
print(global_count)   # Output depends on how many
times the function was called
Use code with caution.
content_copy
```

.

By following these principles and considerations, you can design pure functions that make your functional code more predictable, easier to test, and suitable for parallel execution. Pure functions are a cornerstone of functional programming and contribute to building clean, reliable, and maintainable software.

3.3 Reasoning About Pure Functions

In functional programming, reasoning about code becomes significantly easier thanks to pure functions. Pure functions, by their very nature, exhibit characteristics that make them predictable and clear in their behavior. Here's how understanding pure functions aids in reasoning about your code:

Deterministic Output: A core principle of pure functions is that they always return the same output for a given set of inputs. This determinism allows you to predict the outcome of a function call with certainty. If you know the inputs, you know exactly what the function will produce. This predictability makes it much easier to trace the flow of data through your program and understand how different parts interact.

Referential Transparency: Referential transparency essentially means that you can replace a call to a pure function with its return value without affecting the program's behavior. Because pure functions rely solely on their inputs and don't produce side effects, their output can be viewed as interchangeable with the function call itself in certain contexts. This transparency allows you to simplify your reasoning about code that uses pure functions. You can focus on the data flowing through the program without worrying about hidden side effects or unexpected changes to global state.

Isolation for Testing: The predictability and lack of side effects in pure functions make them ideal candidates for unit testing. You can isolate a pure function with specific test inputs and verify its output. Since the function's behavior is always the same for those inputs, you can have high confidence in the correctness of your tests. This isolation of concerns makes testing functional code more efficient and reliable.

Composability: Pure functions are often designed to be composable. This means you can combine multiple pure functions to create more complex logic. Because the functions are pure, you can reason about the overall behavior by understanding the behavior of each individual function. You can break down a complex problem into smaller, well-defined pure functions and then chain them together. Reasoning about the correctness of the entire chain becomes a matter of understanding each step and how the outputs of one function feed into the inputs of the next.

Here's an example to illustrate reasoning with pure functions:

Python
```python
def add(x, y):
  """Returns the sum of two numbers."""
  return x + y


def multiply(x, y):
  """Returns the product of two numbers."""
  return x * y


result = add(multiply(2, 3), 5)  # result will be 11


# Reasoning about the code:
* We know `multiply(2, 3)` will always return 6.
* Because `add` is pure, we can reason that `add(6, 5)` is
equivalent to simply substituting 6 for the function call.
* Therefore, the final result (`result`) will be 6 + 5 = 11.
```

In this example, our reasoning relies on the fact that both `add` and `multiply` are pure functions. We can break down the nested function calls into their constituent parts and reason about the final outcome with confidence.

By understanding and leveraging the reasoning benefits of pure functions, you can write functional code that is easier to understand, debug, and maintain. The predictability and composability of pure functions promote a style of programming that is clear, concise, and fosters better code reliability.

Use code with caution.

content_copy

Part 2: Core Functional Techniques

Chapter 4
Functional Data Structures

,Functional programming relies heavily on functional data structures. These are data structures specifically designed to be immutable, meaning their contents cannot be modified after creation. This immutability aligns perfectly with the principles of pure functions and helps create predictable and reliable code.

Here's a deeper dive into functional data structures:

Why Immutability Matters:

Predictable Behavior: Since functional data structures are immutable, their state remains constant. This eliminates the complexity of tracking potential mutations throughout your code and ensures consistent behavior.

Reduced Bugs: Mutable data structures can lead to bugs caused by unintended side effects. Immutability eliminates this risk. When you need to make changes, you create a new data structure with the modifications, leaving the original intact.

Enhanced Thread Safety: In multithreaded environments, immutability avoids the need for complex synchronization mechanisms to prevent race conditions. Each thread works with its own copy of the data, simplifying concurrent programming.

Common Functional Data Structures:

Lists: Functional languages often provide immutable lists that offer operations like adding or removing elements without modifying the original list. Instead, a new list with the changes is returned.

Sets: Immutable sets provide functionality for adding, removing, and checking elements for membership, all while maintaining an immutable set representation.

Maps: Functional maps, also known as dictionaries, offer key-value pairings where the keys uniquely identify values. Operations like inserting, retrieving, or removing key-value pairs result in new maps, keeping the original map intact.

Trees: Immutable tree structures can represent hierarchical data. Operations like insertions or deletions create new trees with the modifications.

Benefits of Functional Data Structures:

Improved Reasoning: Immutability makes reasoning about program state simpler. You can focus on how the data structures are transformed without worrying about unexpected changes.

Enhanced Testability: Since functional data structures and the operations on them are often pure, testing becomes more straightforward. You can isolate operations and have confidence in the expected outcomes.

Potential Performance Optimizations: In some cases, functional data structures can lead to performance optimizations. Since immutability allows for sharing of underlying data structures when no changes are made, functional languages can sometimes avoid unnecessary copying compared to mutable data structures.

Functional Data Structures in Python:

While Python itself doesn't enforce immutability by default, libraries like immutablecollections provide functional data structures like lists, sets, and dictionaries that are immutable. These libraries offer a way to work with functional data structures even in a language like Python.

In conclusion, functional data structures are a cornerstone of functional programming. Their immutability fosters a style of programming that is clear, reliable, and easier to reason about. By leveraging these data structures, you can write functional code that is more predictable, less error-prone, and suitable for concurrent programming.

.4.1 Lists, Tuples, and Sets in Functional Programming

In functional programming, lists, tuples, and sets are fundamental data structures used to store and organize collections of elements. However, unlike their counterparts in imperative programming, functional languages often emphasize immutability, meaning the contents of these data structures cannot be modified after creation. This focus on immutability aligns with core functional programming principles like pure functions and simplifies reasoning about program state.

Here's a breakdown of these common data structures in the context of functional programming:

1. Lists:

Functional lists are similar to traditional lists but are immutable. You can't change the elements within a list after it's created.

To modify a list, you create a new list with the desired changes. This promotes immutability and avoids unexpected side effects.

Common operations on functional lists include adding or removing elements, finding elements, and iterating over the elements. These operations typically return a new list reflecting the changes or the desired results, rather than modifying the original list.

2. Tuples:

Tuples are another fundamental data structure, similar to lists but completely immutable. They offer a fixed-size collection of elements once created.

Tuples are ideal for representing data that shouldn't change, like configuration settings or coordinates.

Since tuples are immutable, there are no operations to add or remove elements. Operations like accessing elements by index or iterating over the elements are common.

3. Sets:

Sets are unordered collections of unique elements. Functional sets are also immutable, ensuring the elements remain unique and don't change after creation. Sets are useful for representing collections where only distinct elements matter, like storing unique identifiers or removing duplicates from a list.
Common operations on functional sets include adding or removing elements, checking for membership, and creating unions or intersections of sets. These operations typically result in new sets with the changes applied.

Benefits of Using Immutable Lists, Tuples, and Sets:

Reasoning about Program State: Immutability simplifies reasoning about program state. You can track how data is transformed through operations without worrying about unexpected side effects that can modify existing data structures.

Reduced Bugs: The absence of mutations helps prevent bugs caused by unintended changes to data. If you need to modify a collection, you create a new one, reducing the risk of errors.

Enhanced Thread Safety: In multithreaded environments, immutability avoids the need for complex synchronization mechanisms like locks to prevent race conditions. Each thread works with its own copy of the data, improving concurrency safety.

In essence, lists, tuples, and sets in functional programming serve the same purpose of storing collections as their mutable counterparts in imperative programming. However, the focus on immutability brings numerous advantages for reasoning, reducing bugs, and enhancing thread safety in functional programs.

4.2 Immutability with Functional Data Structures

Immutability and functional data structures go hand-in-hand in functional programming. It's a powerful combination that promotes predictable, reliable, and easier-to-reason-about code. Here's how immutability strengthens functional data structures:

Core Principle: Immutable By Design

Functional data structures are designed to be immutable from the ground up. This means their contents cannot be modified after they are created.

Unlike mutable data structures in imperative programming, where elements can be changed in-place, functional data structures offer operations that create new data structures with the desired modifications.

Benefits of Immutability:

Simpler Reasoning About Program State: When data structures are immutable, their state remains constant throughout the program's execution. This eliminates the mental overhead of tracking potential mutations and reasoning about how changes in one part of the code might affect other parts that rely on the same data.

Reduced Bugs from Side Effects: Mutable data structures can lead to unintended side effects. Imagine a function that modifies a list you're using elsewhere in your code. This can cause unexpected behavior and bugs that are difficult to track down. Immutability eliminates this risk. When you need to make changes, you create a new data structure, leaving the original intact. This ensures that other parts of your code that rely on the original data are not affected by the modifications.

Enhanced Thread Safety: In multithreaded environments, where multiple threads can access and modify data simultaneously, immutability shines. Mutable data structures require complex synchronization mechanisms (like locks) to prevent race conditions where threads overwrite each other's changes. By using immutable data structures, you eliminate the need for these mechanisms altogether. Since each thread works with its own copy of the data, there's no risk of conflicts, simplifying concurrent programming and reducing the potential for thread-related errors.

Functional Data Structure Examples:

Immutable Lists: Functional languages like Haskell or Scala provide immutable lists. Instead of modifying an existing list, functions like cons (prepend) or append create new lists with the elements you want to add or remove.

Immutable Sets: Similar to lists, functional sets are also immutable. Adding or removing elements from a set results in a new set with the changes applied.

Persistent Data Structures: Some functional languages offer persistent data structures. These are immutable structures that share underlying data whenever possible. This allows for efficient creation of new data structures with modifications while avoiding unnecessary copying of unchanged data.

Immutability and Pure Functions:

Immutability complements pure functions, another cornerstone of functional programming. Pure functions don't produce side effects and rely solely on their inputs to produce an output. Since immutable data structures don't have side effects by nature (their state cannot be changed), they align perfectly with the principles of pure functions. This creates a powerful combination for writing predictable and reliable functional code.

In conclusion, immutability is not just an incidental property of functional data structures; it's a deliberate design choice that yields significant benefits for functional programming. By embracing immutability, you can write code that is easier to reason about, less error-prone, suitable for concurrent programming, and promotes a more declarative style of programming.

4.3 Working with Records and Custom Data Types

.

Functional programming languages offer powerful mechanisms for working with records and custom data types. These features allow you to structure your data in a meaningful way, improving code readability, maintainability, and type safety.

Records

Records are a fundamental data structure in many functional languages. They act like containers that group related pieces of data under a single name.
Similar to structs in other languages, records typically consist of named fields that can hold different data types.
Benefits of Records:

Improved Readability: Records make your code more readable by clearly defining the structure of your data with named fields. This clarity becomes especially important when dealing with complex data that has multiple attributes.
Type Safety: Many functional languages enforce type safety for record fields. This ensures data integrity by guaranteeing that each field holds the expected data type. This helps catch errors early in the development process.

Immutability: Records can be designed to be immutable, aligning well with functional programming principles. This means the data within a record cannot be modified after creation.

Example (Record in Haskell):

Haskell
```
data Person = Person { name :: String, age :: Int }

person1 = Person "Alice" 30
```
Use code with caution.

content_copy

In this example, the Person record definition specifies two fields: name (string) and age (integer). The person1 variable creates a record instance with specific values for those fields.

Custom Data Types

Functional languages often allow you to define custom data types beyond built-in primitives like records. These custom types can encapsulate complex data structures and logic, promoting code reusability and maintainability.

Benefits of Custom Data Types:

Code Reusability: By defining custom data types, you can encapsulate functionality specific to that data type. This allows you to reuse the same logic for working with that data type throughout your code.

Improved Maintainability: Well-designed custom data types can improve code maintainability by centralizing logic and data structure definitions. If you need to modify how you work with that data, you can make changes within the custom data type definition, reducing the need to alter code scattered throughout your program.

Stronger Type Safety: Custom data types can enforce stricter type checking, leading to more robust and reliable code.

Example (Maybe type in Haskell):

Haskell

```
data Maybe a = Nothing | Just a
```

```
getValue :: Maybe String -> String
getValue Nothing = "No value present"
getValue (Just value) = value
```
Use code with caution.

content_copy

The Maybe type is a common example of a custom data type in Haskell. It represents an optional value. It can either be Nothing (indicating no value) or Just a (where a is any data type). The getValue function demonstrates how to handle the different cases of the Maybe type.

Working with Records and Custom Data Types Effectively:

Choose meaningful names for records and custom data types to enhance readability.

Leverage type safety features to ensure data integrity.

Design custom data types to encapsulate relevant functionality and data structures.

By effectively using records and custom data types, you can write functional code that is clear, maintainable, type-safe, and promotes better code organization.

Chapter 5

Functional Iteration and Recursion

Functional programming offers two primary approaches to iterating over data and performing repetitive tasks: recursion and higher-order functions. Both methods can achieve iteration without using explicit loops like for or while loops found in imperative programming.

1. Recursion:

Recursion is a technique where a function calls itself within its body. This allows you to break down a problem into smaller, similar subproblems until you reach a base case that can be solved directly.

Recursion can be a natural fit for functional programming because it avoids the need for mutable state variables and loops.

Example (Factorial function in Python):

```python
Python
def factorial(n):
    """Calculates the factorial of a number."""
```

```
if n == 0:
  return 1
else:
  return n * factorial(n-1)
```

```
result = factorial(5)  # result will be 120
```
Use code with caution.

content_copy

In this example, the factorial function recursively calls itself with a decrementing value of n until it reaches the base case of n == 0.

2. Higher-Order Functions:

Higher-order functions are functions that take other functions as arguments or return functions as results. They provide a powerful way to abstract over common iteration patterns without explicit loops.

Functional languages offer built-in higher-order functions like map, filter, reduce, and fold that can be used for various iteration tasks.

Example (Using map in Python):

Python

```python
numbers = [1, 2, 3, 4]
squared_numbers = list(map(lambda x: x * x, numbers)) #
Map applies a function to each element
print(squared_numbers) # Output: [1, 4, 9, 16]
```

Use code with caution.

content_copy

Here, the map function applies a lambda expression (a concise anonymous function) that squares each element in the numbers list. Higher-order functions like filter can be used to filter elements based on a condition, and reduce can be used to accumulate elements into a single value.

Choosing Between Recursion and Higher-Order Functions:

While both recursion and higher-order functions can be used for iteration, there are some general guidelines to consider:

For simpler iteration tasks, higher-order functions like map and filter are often preferred due to their readability and potential for performance optimizations.

Recursion can be a good choice for problems that naturally divide into smaller subproblems of the same form. It can also lead to more concise code in some cases.

In conclusion, functional programming offers recursion and higher-order functions as powerful tools for iterating over data. Understanding these techniques allows you to write concise, declarative code without relying on mutable state or explicit loops.

Sources

info

www.reddit.com/user/ELITESLAYER10/comments/11cd o2w/hashnode_blog/

5.1 List Comprehensions and Generator Expressions

List comprehensions and generator expressions are both powerful tools in Python for creating new lists based on existing data. While they achieve a similar outcome, they differ in their approach and use cases.

List Comprehensions:

List comprehensions provide a concise way to create a new list based on an existing iterable.

They use a readable syntax that combines iterating over an iterable, applying a conditional statement (optional), and potentially performing a transformation on each element.

The result is a new list containing the elements that meet the conditions and have undergone the specified transformations.

Syntax:

Python
new_list = [expression for item in iterable if condition]
Use code with caution.

content_copy

expression: This defines what to do with each element in the iterable. It can be a simple variable reference, a mathematical operation, or a function call.

item: This represents the variable used to access each element during iteration.

iterable: This is the data source you want to iterate over, such as a list, tuple, or string.

condition (optional): This is a Boolean expression that filters the elements in the iterable. Only elements that evaluate to True are included in the new list.

Example:

Python
numbers = [1, 2, 3, 4, 5]
squared_numbers = [num * num for num in numbers] #
Square each number
even_numbers = [num for num in numbers if num % 2 ==
0] # Filter even numbers
Use code with caution.
content_copy

Generator Expressions:

Generator expressions are similar to list comprehensions, but they are more memory-efficient. Instead of creating a new list in memory all at once, generator expressions yield elements on demand, one at a time. This is useful for working with very large datasets or when you only need to iterate over the elements once.

Syntax:

Python
```
generator = (expression for item in iterable if condition)
```
Use code with caution.

content_copy

The syntax is very similar to list comprehensions, but the result is a generator object instead of a list.

Example:

Python
```
large_numbers = range(1000000)  # Large list of numbers

# Using list comprehension (might be memory intensive)
squared_numbers_list = [num * num for num in large_numbers]

# Using generator expression (more memory efficient)
squared_numbers_generator = (num * num for num in large_numbers)
```

```
# Iterate over the generator
for num in squared_numbers_generator:
  print(num)  # Process each number as it's generated
```
Use code with caution.

content_copy

Choosing Between List Comprehensions and Generator Expressions:

Use list comprehensions when:

You need the entire result stored as a list in memory for further processing.

The data you're working with is relatively small and memory usage isn't a concern.

The code readability benefits of list comprehensions outweigh the potential memory efficiency gains of generator expressions (for smaller datasets).

Use generator expressions when:

You're working with very large datasets and memory efficiency is crucial.

You only need to iterate over the elements once and don't need to store the entire result in memory.

In essence, both list comprehensions and generator expressions offer concise ways to create new lists in Python. Understanding their strengths and use cases will help you choose the right tool for your specific needs.

5.2 Functional Iteration with map, filter, and reduce

Functional programming offers a powerful approach to iterating over data without relying on explicit loops like for or while. This is achieved through higher-order functions, functions that operate on other functions. Three fundamental functions in this category are map, filter, and reduce. Let's explore how they work for functional iteration:

1. map:

Purpose: Applies a function to each element of an iterable (list, tuple, etc.) and returns a new iterable with the results.

Benefits:

Conciseness: Avoids explicit loops, leading to cleaner and more readable code.

Parallelization Potential: In some functional languages, map can be parallelized for improved performance on large datasets.

Example (Python):

Python

```
numbers = [1, 2, 3, 4]
squared_numbers = list(map(lambda x: x * x, numbers))  #
Map applies a lambda function
print(squared_numbers)  # Output: [1, 4, 9, 16]
```

Use code with caution.

content_copy

2. filter:

Purpose: Creates a new iterable containing only elements from the original iterable that pass a certain condition.

Benefits:

Readability: Clearly expresses the filtering logic for selecting elements.

Reusability: The filtering logic can be encapsulated in a separate function for reuse.

Example (Python):

Python

```
numbers = [1, 2, 3, 4, 5]
even_numbers = list(filter(lambda x: x % 2 == 0, numbers))
print(even_numbers)  # Output: [2, 4]
```

Use code with caution.

content_copy

3. reduce:

Purpose: Accumulates elements of an iterable into a single value using a provided function.

Benefits:

Conciseness: Offers a compact way to perform complex aggregations without loops.

Functional Style: Aligns with the functional programming paradigm of reducing complex operations to simpler function applications.

Example (Python - using functools module):

Python

```
from functools import reduce

numbers = [1, 2, 3, 4]
total = reduce(lambda x, y: x + y, numbers)
print(total)  # Output: 10
```

Use code with caution.

content_copy

Key Points:

These functions are often used in combination for more complex functional iteration tasks.

They promote immutability, as they typically create new iterables rather than modifying existing ones.

Functional languages may offer built-in versions of these functions or similar abstractions.

In conclusion, map, filter, and reduce provide powerful tools for functional iteration. By leveraging these higher-order functions, you can write cleaner, more concise, and declarative code for processing data in functional programming paradigms.

5.3 Power of Recursion in Functional Programming

Recursion is a powerful technique that shines in functional programming due to its ability to solve problems by breaking them down into smaller, self-similar subproblems. This approach aligns well with the core principles of functional programming, offering several advantages:

Elegance and Simplicity: Recursive functions can often express complex problems in a concise and intuitive way. The structure of the function mirrors the structure of the problem itself, leading to clear and readable code.

Immutability: Functional programming emphasizes immutability, where data structures are not modified after creation. Recursion naturally fits into this paradigm. Instead of mutating existing data, a recursive function typically creates new data structures with the desired modifications.

Tail Recursion Optimization: In some cases, functional programming languages can optimize tail recursion. Tail recursion occurs when the recursive call is the last expression evaluated in a function. Through optimization, these tail-recursive functions can avoid the overhead of function call stacks, making them efficient for certain problems.

Natural Fit for Data Structures: Recursion often proves to be a natural way to work with hierarchical data structures like trees or linked lists. By recursively traversing these structures, you can elegantly process each node or element without complex loops.

Here's a classic example of recursion in functional programming:

```python
Python
def factorial(n):
```

```python
    """Calculates the factorial of a number using recursion."""
    if n == 0:
      return 1
    else:
      return n * factorial(n-1)


# Example usage
result = factorial(5)
print(result)  # Output: 120
```
Use code with caution.

content_copy

In this example, the factorial function breaks down the problem of calculating the factorial (n!) into smaller subproblems, recursively multiplying n by the factorial of n-1 until it reaches the base case of n being 0.

Functional vs. Imperative Recursion:

It's important to note that recursion can also be used in imperative programming styles. However, functional recursion aligns better with immutability and avoids the potential side effects that can arise from mutable state variables in imperative approaches.

When to Consider Recursion:

While recursion offers elegance and can be a natural fit for certain problems, it's not always the most efficient approach. Here are some general guidelines:

If there's a clear iterative solution (using loops) that might be more performant, especially for very large datasets, consider an iterative approach.

Tail recursion is generally preferred over head recursion (where the recursive call happens before other computations in the function) due to potential optimization benefits.

In conclusion, recursion is a powerful tool in the functional programmer's toolbox. Its ability to decompose problems, promote immutability, and often lead to concise code makes it a valuable technique for various functional programming tasks.

Chapter 6

Monads and Functors (Optional)

In functional programming, functors and monads are two advanced concepts that deal with applying functions to values and handling contextual data. While they may seem complex at first, they offer powerful tools for structuring and composing functional programs.

Functors:

Core Idea: Functors provide a way to apply functions to values wrapped in a specific context. They don't modify the underlying value but rather create a new value with the applied function.

Think of it as: A wrapper around a value that can be manipulated by functions specifically designed for that wrapper type.

Benefits:

Abstraction: Functors provide a layer of abstraction over different data types, allowing you to work with them uniformly through the map function.

Code Reusability: Functions designed to work with functors can be reused across different data types that share the same underlying context.

Example (Maybe Monad as a Functor in Haskell):

Haskell
data Maybe a = Nothing | Just a

```
myFunctor :: (a -> b) -> Maybe a -> Maybe b
myFunctor f Nothing  = Nothing
myFunctor f (Just a) = Just (f a)
```

```
# Applying a function to a Maybe value (Just 5)
result = myFunctor (* 2) (Just 5)  -- result will be Just 10
```
Use code with caution.
content_copy

In this example, Maybe acts as a functor. The myFunctor function applies the provided function f to the value wrapped in Maybe, considering the context of potentially missing values (represented by Nothing).

Monads:

Building on Functors: Monads extend the concept of functors by adding the ability to chain computations and handle effects (like error handling or working with input/output) in a functional style.

Think of it as: A special kind of functor that can also sequence computations and manage contextual data.

Benefits:

Monad Transformers: Functional languages often provide monad transformers that allow you to compose multiple monadic effects (like error handling and logging) cleanly.

Expressive Power: Monads enable you to write more expressive functional code that deals with effects in a controlled manner.

Example (Maybe Monad for Handling Potential Errors):

Haskell

```
data Maybe a = Nothing | Just a

divide :: Int -> Maybe Int
divide 0 _ = Nothing
divide divisor dividend = Just (dividend `div` divisor)

safeDivision :: Int -> Int -> Maybe Int
```

```
safeDivision divisor dividend = maybe Nothing (Just)
(divide divisor dividend)

# Chaining computations with Maybe monad
result = safeDivision 10 0 >>= (* 2)   -- result will be
Nothing (error handling)
Use code with caution.
```

content_copy

Here, the Maybe monad is used not only to represent optional values but also to handle potential division by zero errors. The safeDivision function returns Nothing if the divisor is zero, and the >>= operator allows chaining computations while considering potential failures.

Monads vs. Functors:

Every monad is a functor, but not every functor is a monad.

Functors deal with applying functions to contextual values, while monads add the ability to chain computations and manage effects.

In conclusion, functors and monads provide powerful abstractions for functional programming. Functors offer a way to work with contextual data, and monads extend that functionality to handle computations and effects in a controlled manner. While they have a learning curve, understanding these concepts can lead to more expressive, reusable, and composable functional code.

6.1 Introduction to Monads and Functors

In functional programming, functors and monads are two advanced concepts that deal with transforming data and handling context. They can be a bit tricky to grasp at first, but they offer powerful tools for building well-structured and composable functional programs. Here's a breakdown to get you started:

Functors: Wrapping Values with Context

Imagine a functor as a special box. This box can hold a value of any type, but it also provides context for that value.

Functors don't modify the underlying value itself. Instead, they provide a way to apply functions to the value while considering the context.

Think of it like having special tools designed to work with these boxes. You can use these tools to manipulate the value inside without opening the box and potentially messing things up.

Benefits of Functors:

Abstraction: Functors provide a layer of abstraction over different data types. This allows you to write generic functions that can work with any type of value wrapped in a specific functor, promoting code reusability.

Uniformity: By using functors, you can treat different data types with similar contexts in a consistent way. This simplifies code and improves readability.

Example: Maybe Monad as a Functor (Haskell)

In some languages like Haskell, the Maybe type acts as a functor. It's a wrapper that can hold a value or indicate that there's no value (Nothing).

Haskell
data Maybe a = Nothing | Just a

```
-- Function to apply to a Maybe value
myFunctor :: (a -> b) -> Maybe a -> Maybe b
myFunctor f Nothing  = Nothing
myFunctor f (Just a) = Just (f a)
```

```
# Applying a function (* 2) to a Maybe value (Just 5)
result = myFunctor (* 2) (Just 5) -- result will be Just 10
```
Use code with caution.
content_copy

Here, the myFunctor function takes a function and a Maybe value. If the Maybe value is Nothing (no value), it returns Nothing. Otherwise, it applies the function to the value inside the Just constructor and wraps the result back in Just.

Monads: Functors with Superpowers

Monads build on top of functors. They are like functors with extra abilities.

In addition to applying functions, monads allow you to chain computations and manage effects in a functional style.

Effects can be things like error handling, working with input/output (like reading from a file), or managing state.

Benefits of Monads:

Composing Computations: Monads allow you to chain multiple operations together, building complex functional programs in a modular way.

Controlled Effects: Monads provide a way to handle effects in a controlled manner, avoiding the pitfalls of side effects that can plague imperative programming.

Monad Transformers: Some languages offer monad transformers. These allow you to combine multiple monadic effects (like error handling and logging) cleanly without cluttering your code.

Example: Maybe Monad for Handling Errors (Haskell)

The Maybe monad can be used not just for optional values but also for error handling.

Haskell

```
data Maybe a = Nothing | Just a

divide :: Int -> Maybe Int
divide 0 _ = Nothing
divide divisor dividend = Just (dividend `div` divisor)

safeDivision :: Int -> Int -> Maybe Int
safeDivision divisor dividend = maybe Nothing (Just)
(divide divisor dividend)
```

Chaining computations with Maybe monad (potential error)

```
result = safeDivision 10 0 >>= (* 2)   -- result will be
Nothing (error handling)
```

Use code with caution.

content_copy

Here, the safeDivision function uses the Maybe monad to return Nothing if there's an error (division by zero). The >>= operator allows chaining computations while considering potential failures. If the division is successful, the result is wrapped in Just and then multiplied by 2.

Monads vs. Functors: A Quick Recap

Every monad is a functor, but not every functor is a monad.
Functors provide a way to apply functions to contextual values.
Monads extend that functionality to handle computations and effects in a controlled manner.

In essence, functors and monads are powerful tools for functional programming. While they have a learning curve, understanding these concepts can lead to more expressive, reusable, and composable functional code.

6.2 Practical Applications of Monads and Functors (focus on common use cases)

Functors and monads, while powerful concepts in functional programming, can seem theoretical at first. But they have practical applications that can improve the structure, readability, and maintainability of your code. Here are some common use cases for functors and monads:

Functors:

Optional Values: Perhaps the most common use case for functors is handling optional values. In many languages, the Maybe monad (or similar concept) acts as a functor. It can hold a value or indicate the absence of a value (Nothing). This helps avoid null pointer exceptions and makes code that deals with potentially missing data more explicit.

Applying Functions with Context: Functors allow you to apply functions to values while considering their context. For example, a list functor might provide functions for filtering elements based on specific criteria or transforming elements while maintaining their position within the list.

Parsing and Validation: Functors can be used to represent the intermediate results of parsing or validation processes. This allows you to accumulate errors or warnings along the way without modifying the original data.

Monads:

Error Handling: Monads like Maybe or Either (which can hold either a value or an error) provide a structured way to handle errors in functional programs. You can chain computations and propagate errors explicitly, making your code more robust.

Asynchronous Programming: In some languages, monads like IO or Task are used to represent asynchronous operations. These monads encapsulate the details of dealing with asynchronous behavior, allowing you to write code that appears sequential but executes asynchronously.

State Management: While functional programming avoids mutable state by default, monads like State can be used to manage state in a controlled manner. This can be useful for specific scenarios where some form of state is necessary.

Here's an example (using Python with optional libraries):

Python
```python
from typing import Optional  # Optional type hint for Maybe-like behavior

# Maybe-like function to handle potential division by zero
def safe_division(divisor: int, dividend: int) -> Optional[int]:
    if divisor == 0:
        return None  # Indicate error (no value)
```

```
    return dividend / divisor

# Using safe_division with type hinting
result: Optional[int] = safe_division(10, 2)   # Optional
type for potential None
if result is not None:
    print(result)  # Output: 5
```
Use code with caution.

content_copy

In this example, the safe_division function uses type hinting to indicate that it might return None (similar to Nothing in some languages). This makes the code more explicit about handling potential errors.

Remember:

Functors and monads can have different implementations in various languages. Grasping the core concepts is more important than memorizing specific syntax.

These concepts can take time to master. Start with simpler use cases and gradually work your way up to more complex scenarios.

By understanding functors and monads, you can write more functional code that is:

Expressive: You can clearly communicate the intent of your code and how it handles different situations (like errors or missing data).

Reusable: Functions designed to work with functors or monads can be reused across different data types with similar contexts.

Composable: Monads allow you to chain operations together, building complex programs from smaller, well-defined functions.

While they may require some investment upfront, functors and monads can be valuable tools for building robust and maintainable functional programs.

Part 3: Advanced Functional Concepts

Chapter 7

Functional Error Handling

Functional programming offers a distinct approach to error handling compared to imperative programming. Here's a breakdown of key concepts involved in functional error handling:

1. Immutability and Avoiding Side Effects:

Functional programming emphasizes immutability, where data structures are not modified after creation. This eliminates the risk of errors caused by unexpected mutations during program execution.

Functional error handling often relies on returning specific values or data structures to indicate errors. This approach avoids side effects like throwing exceptions (which can disrupt program flow) or modifying global error state variables.

2. Error Handling with Optional Types:

Many functional languages offer optional type systems like Maybe (Haskell) or Option (Scala) to represent the potential absence of a value.

A function that might encounter missing data can return the data wrapped in the optional type or an empty variant of the optional type (like Nothing in Maybe) to signal an error.

Example (Maybe Monad for Error Handling in Haskell):

Haskell

```
data Maybe a = Nothing | Just a

divide :: Int -> Maybe Int
divide 0 _ = Nothing
divide divisor dividend = Just (dividend `div` divisor)

safeDivision :: Int -> Int -> Maybe Int
safeDivision divisor dividend = maybe Nothing (Just)
(divide divisor dividend)
```

Use code with caution.

content_copy

In this example, the divide function might return Nothing if there's a division by zero error. The safeDivision function utilizes the Maybe monad to handle this potential error.

3. Pattern Matching for Handling Errors:

Functional languages often rely on pattern matching to handle different cases in a function's output. This includes checking for error states represented by specific values or data structures.

Example (Pattern Matching in Haskell):

```Haskell
calculateArea :: Maybe Float -> Maybe Float
calculateArea Nothing = Nothing
calculateArea (Just side) = Just (side * side)

# Usage with pattern matching
result <- calculateArea (Just 5.0)   -- result will be Just 25.0
result <- calculateArea Nothing      -- result will be Nothing (error handling)
```

Use code with caution.

content_copy

Here, the calculateArea function uses pattern matching to differentiate between a Just value (containing the side length) and Nothing (indicating an error).

4. Monads for Complex Error Handling:

Monads like Either (which can hold a value or an error) can be used for more complex error handling scenarios. The Either monad allows you to represent both successful computations (containing a value) and failures (containing an error value).

Example (Either Monad for Errors in Haskell):

Haskell

```
data Either String Int = Left String | Right Int

parseInt :: String -> Either String Int
parseInt str = case reads str :: [(Int, String)] of
  [] -> Left "Invalid integer format"
  [(value, "")] -> Right value
  _ -> Left "Multiple interpretations"
```

```
# Usage with pattern matching
result <- parseInt "123" -- result will be Right 123
result <- parseInt "abc"  -- result will be Left "Invalid
integer format"
Use code with caution.
```

content_copy

The parseInt function uses the Either monad to return either the parsed integer (Right) or an error message (Left) based on the input string.

Benefits of Functional Error Handling:

Immutability: Reduces errors caused by side effects and unexpected data mutations.

Explicit Error Handling: Forces you to explicitly consider and handle potential errors in your code.

Composability: Functions can be composed without worrying about unexpected exceptions interrupting program flow.

Conclusion:

Functional error handling offers a robust and predictable approach to managing errors in your programs. By leveraging immutability, optional types, pattern matching, and monads, you can write functional code that is clear, reliable, and easier to reason about.

7.1 Traditional Error Handling vs. Functional Approach

Traditional error handling and functional error handling take different approaches to managing errors in a program. Here's a breakdown of the key differences:

Traditional Error Handling:

Approach: Often relies on exceptions or error codes to signal errors during program execution.
Code Flow Disruption: Exceptions can abruptly halt program flow, requiring try-catch blocks or error handling mechanisms to resume execution.

Side Effects: Error handling might involve modifying global state variables or printing error messages, introducing potential side effects.

Error Checking: The onus is often on the programmer to explicitly check for errors (e.g., null pointer checks) throughout the code.

Example (Python with try-except):

Python
```
def divide(numerator, denominator):
  """Divides two numbers and handles potential division by zero error using try-except."""
  try:
    return numerator / denominator
  except ZeroDivisionError:
    print("Error: Cannot divide by zero.")
    return None  # Or raise a custom exception


result = divide(10, 2)
print(result)  # Output: 5.0


result = divide(10, 0)
print(result)  # Output: Error: Cannot divide by zero.
```

```
#       None
```
Use code with caution.

content_copy

Functional Error Handling:

Approach: Leverages data types and functions to represent and handle errors.

Focus on Values: Functions return specific values or data structures to indicate errors, avoiding disrupting program flow.

Immutability: Functional programming emphasizes immutability, reducing errors caused by side effects during error handling.

Error Propagation: Errors are often propagated through the code by returning specific error values, making error handling more explicit.

Example (Python with Optional Types):

Python
```python
from typing import Optional
```

```python
def safe_division(numerator: int, denominator: int) ->
Optional[int]:
  """Divides two numbers and returns None if there's a
division by zero error."""
  if denominator == 0:
    return None
  return numerator / denominator

result = safe_division(10, 2)
print(result)  # Output: 5.0

result = safe_division(10, 0)
print(result)  # Output: None
```
Use code with caution.
content_copy

Choosing Between Traditional and Functional
Approaches:

Traditional: Suitable for existing codebases or when
exceptions offer a clear way to handle errors (e.g.,
network errors).

Functional: Well-suited for new functional programs where immutability and explicit error handling are desirable.

Key Benefits of Functional Error Handling:

Immutability: Reduces errors caused by side effects.

Composability: Functions can be easily combined without worrying about exceptions interrupting the flow.

Expressive: Code clearly indicates how errors are handled and propagated.

Easier Reasoning: Reasoning about error handling logic can be simpler due to the absence of side effects.

In conclusion, both traditional and functional error handling have their merits. Understanding these approaches can help you choose the most suitable technique for your specific programming paradigm and project requirements.

7.2 Using Exceptions in Functional Programming

Functional programming generally discourages the use of exceptions for error handling due to several reasons:

Disrupting Program Flow: Exceptions can abruptly halt program execution, making reasoning about code behavior more challenging. Functional programming favors predictable control flow.

Side Effects: Traditional exception handling might involve side effects like modifying global state or printing error messages, which can be difficult to reason about and can lead to unexpected behavior.

Immutability: Functional programming emphasizes immutability, where data structures are not modified after creation. Exceptions can sometimes lead to unintended mutations during error handling.

However, there are some situations where exceptions might be considered in functional programming, but with caution:

Unexpected Errors: For truly unexpected errors that halt the entire program (e.g., system errors, out-of-memory exceptions), exceptions might be used as a last resort to signal these errors.

Interfacing with External Code: If you're working with external libraries or code written in imperative languages that rely on exceptions, you might need to handle those exceptions within your functional code to ensure proper integration.

Alternatives to Exceptions in Functional Programming:

Optional Types: Many functional languages offer optional type systems like Maybe (Haskell) or Option (Scala) to represent the potential absence of a value. Functions can return the data wrapped in the optional type or an empty variant to indicate an error.

Monads: Monads like Either (which can hold a value or an error) can be used for more complex error handling scenarios. The Either monad allows you to represent both successful computations (containing a value) and failures (containing an error value).

Pattern Matching: Functional languages often rely on pattern matching to handle different cases in a function's output. This includes checking for error states represented by specific values or data structures.

Here's a quick comparison:

https://docs.google.com/spreadsheets/d/1kG-ULO970FD hVqfFeCudPF5SA7j8mfHUgHwsQA5tATU/edit?usp=dri vesdk

Export to Sheets

In essence, while exceptions might be used in specific cases, functional programming offers a range of techniques for robust error handling that promote immutability, composability, and clearer reasoning about program behavior.

7.2 Using Exceptions in Functional Programming

In functional programming, exceptions are generally discouraged for error handling

This stems from the core principles of functional programming, which prioritize predictable behavior and immutability. Here's a breakdown of why exceptions and functional programming don't always mix well, and what alternatives you might consider:

Why Exceptions Clash with Functional Programming:

Disrupted Program Flow: Exceptions can abruptly halt program execution, making it difficult to reason about how the rest of the code should behave.

Functional programming favors a more controlled and predictable flow of data through functions.

Side Effects: Traditional exception handling often involves side effects, like modifying global state or printing error messages. These side effects can be tricky to reason about and can lead to unexpected behavior. Immutability, a core principle in functional programming, discourages such modifications.

Immutability Violations: Exceptions can sometimes lead to unintended mutations during error handling. This can go against the functional programming approach of keeping data structures unchanged after creation. Alternatives to Exceptions in Functional Programming:

Functional programming offers a rich set of tools for handling errors without resorting to exceptions:

Optional Types: Many functional languages provide optional type systems like Maybe (Haskell) or Option (Scala). These represent the potential absence of a value. A function can return either the data wrapped in the optional type or an empty variant (like Nothing in Maybe) to signal an error.

Monads: Monads like Either (which can hold a value or an error) are powerful tools for error handling. The Either monad allows you to represent computations that can either succeed with a value or fail with an error value. Functions can return an Either type, and you can chain computations whileexplicitly handling errors at each step.

Pattern Matching: Functional languages often rely on pattern matching to handle different cases in a function's output. This includes checking for error states represented by specific values or data structures within the returned types (like checking for Nothing in Maybe or the Left variant of Either).

Here's a table summarizing the key differences

https://docs.google.com/spreadsheets/d/1EYz4AuxGEEx2m2eLj4x4r-Iy0aZOjI0jbdOKrME1jNo/edit?usp=drivesdk

Exceptions: Not Entirely Forbidden, But

Use with Caution

While exceptions are generally discouraged, there can be some situations where they might be considered:

Unexpected Errors: For truly unexpected errors that would halt the entire program anyway (e.g., system errors, out-of-memory exceptions), exceptions might be used as a last resort to signal these errors.

Interfacing with External Code: If you're working with external libraries or code written in imperative languages that rely on exceptions, you might need to handle those exceptions within your functional code to ensure proper integration.

In conclusion, exceptions can be used sparingly in functional programming, but understanding their limitations is crucial. Functional programming offers a robust set of techniques for error handling that promote immutability, composability, and clearer reasoning about program behavior.

7.3 Maybe Monad for Handling Optional Values

The Maybe monad is a fundamental concept in functional programming, particularly useful for handling optional values. It provides a way to represent the possibility of a value being absent and allows you to write code that explicitly deals with this possibility.

Core Idea:

Imagine a box (the Maybe monad) that can hold a value of any type or be empty. This box not only stores the value but also the context of its existence. The Maybe monad typically has two constructors:

Just a: This constructor contains the actual value (a) within the Maybe monad.
Nothing: This constructor represents the absence of a value within the Maybe monad.

Benefits of Using Maybe Monad:

Safer Code: By explicitly representing the absence of values, you avoid null pointer exceptions and similar errors that can plague imperative programming.
Improved Readability: Code that uses Maybe monads becomes more readable as it clearly indicates where values might be missing.
Composable Functions: Functions can be written to operate on Maybe monads, allowing you to chain

operations while considering the possibility of missing values at each step.

Example (Maybe Monad in Haskell):

Haskell

```
data Maybe a = Nothing | Just a

-- Function to find the length of a string (if it exists)
safeLength :: Maybe String -> Maybe Int
safeLength Nothing = Nothing
safeLength (Just str) = Just (length str)

# Usage
name = "Alice"
nameLength = safeLength (Just name)   -- result will be
Just 5
noName = Nothing
noNameLength = safeLength noName     -- result will be
Nothing (no value)
```

Use code with caution.

content_copy

In this example, the safeLength function takes a Maybe String and returns a Maybe Int. If the input string is

Nothing (no value), the function also returns Nothing. Otherwise, it applies the length function to the string and wraps the result in Just.

Key Operations on Maybe Monad:

isJust: Checks if the Maybe monad contains a value (returns True for Just a, False for Nothing).
isNothing: Checks if the Maybe monad is empty (returns True for Nothing, False for Just a).
maybe f default: Applies a function f to the contained value if it exists, otherwise returns the provided default value.

In conclusion, the Maybe monad is a powerful tool for handling optional values in functional programming. By leveraging Maybe monads, you can write code that is safer, more readable, and composable, leading to more robust and maintainable functional programs.

Chapter 8
Parallelism and Concurrency with Functional Programming

Functional programming and its principles can align well with parallelism and concurrency, offering potential for performance improvements and efficient utilization of multi-core processors. Here's how functional programming concepts contribute to effective parallel programming:

Immutability and Thread Safety:

Functional programming emphasizes immutability, where data structures are not modified after creation. This eliminates the need for complex synchronization mechanisms (like locks or mutexes) that are often required in imperative programming to avoid data races during parallel execution.

Since functions in functional programming don't have side effects and rely purely on their inputs to produce outputs, they are inherently thread-safe. This means you can execute them concurrently on multiple cores without worrying about unexpected behavior.

Declarative Style and Focus on What:

Functional programming focuses on what needs to be computed rather than how it should be done step-by-step. This allows the compiler or runtime to optimize and potentially parallelize the execution of these computations.

By expressing the problem declaratively, you provide the system with more flexibility to determine the most efficient way to achieve the desired outcome, potentially leveraging multiple cores for parallel execution.

Higher-Order Functions and Abstraction:

Functional programming heavily utilizes higher-order functions, which take functions as arguments or return functions as results. These higher-order functions can be powerful tools for expressing parallel computations in a concise and reusable way.

Libraries and frameworks often provide high-level abstractions for parallel programming using functional concepts. These abstractions can simplify the process of writing parallel functional programs without getting bogged down in low-level details of thread management.

Examples of Parallelism with Functional Programming:

Mapping a function across a list: In many functional languages, libraries provide functions like map that can apply a function to each element of a list in parallel across multiple cores, improving performance for large datasets.

Parallelizing independent computations: Functional code that involves breaking down a problem into smaller, independent tasks is a good candidate for parallelization. These tasks can then be executed concurrently on multiple cores.

Challenges and Considerations:

Identifying Parallelism Opportunities: Not all functional programs are inherently parallelizable. It's crucial to identify sections of code where computations are independent and can be executed concurrently without affecting the overall outcome.

Overhead of Task Creation and Management: While functional code might be thread-safe, creating and managing tasks for parallel execution can introduce some overhead. This overhead needs to be weighed against the potential performance gains from parallelization.

In conclusion, functional programming offers a foundation for effective parallel programming. Immutability, focus on declarativeness, and higher-order functions all contribute to writing code that can be efficiently executed on multi-core processors. However, it's important to carefully evaluate the suitability of your problem for parallelization and consider the potential overhead involved.

8.1 Leveraging Functional Programming for Parallel Processing

The world of multi-core processors demands techniques to harness their full potential. Functional programming, with its emphasis on immutability and pure functions, shines in this area by providing a solid foundation for parallel processing. Here's how functional programming concepts can be leveraged for effective parallel processing:

Immutability and Thread Safety:

Functional programming champions immutability, where data structures are created and remain unchanged throughout the program. This eliminates the need for complex synchronization mechanisms (like locks or mutexes) that plague parallel programming in imperative styles. Since multiple threads can't accidentally modify the same data, functional programs are inherently thread-safe.

Functions, the building blocks of functional programming, are devoid of side effects. They purely rely on their inputs to produce predictable outputs. This makes them inherently thread-safe as well. You can execute them concurrently on multiple cores without worrying about unexpected behavior arising from data races (conflicting writes from different threads).

Declarative Style and Focus on "What"

Functional programming focuses on expressing what needs to be computed, not the nitty-gritty how. This allows compilers or runtime systems to optimize and potentially parallelize the execution of these computations.

By describing the problem declaratively, you provide the system with more flexibility. It can then determine the most efficient way to achieve the desired outcome, potentially leveraging multiple cores for parallel execution. The compiler or runtime can analyze the code and identify opportunities to break down tasks and execute them concurrently.

Higher-Order Functions and Abstraction:

Functional programming thrives on higher-order functions. These functions accept functions as arguments or return functions as results. They act as powerful tools for expressing parallel computations in a concise and reusable way.

Libraries and frameworks often provide high-level abstractions for parallel programming using functional concepts. These abstractions simplify the process of writing parallel functional programs. Instead of getting bogged down in low-level details of thread management, you can focus on the core logic using these abstractions.

Examples of Parallelism with Functional Programming:

Mapping a Function Across a List: Many functional languages offer libraries with functions like map. These functions can apply a function to each element of a large list concurrently across multiple cores. This can significantly improve performance, especially when dealing with massive datasets.

Parallelizing Independent Computations: Functional code that involves breaking down a problem into smaller, independent tasks is a prime candidate for parallelization. These independent tasks can then be executed concurrently on multiple cores, utilizing the processing power effectively.

Challenges and Considerations:

Identifying Parallelism Opportunities: Not all functional programs are inherently parallelizable. It's crucial to identify sections of code where computations are independent and can be executed concurrently without affecting the overall outcome. Not every problem can be neatly divided into independent subtasks.

Overhead of Task Creation and Management: While functional code might be thread-safe, creating and managing tasks for parallel execution can introduce some overhead. This overhead needs to be weighed against the potential performance gains from parallelization. Creating and managing numerous tasks might negate the benefits of parallelization, especially for smaller datasets.

In conclusion, functional programming offers a strong foundation for effective parallel processing. Immutability, focus on declarativeness, and higher-order functions all contribute to writing code that can be efficiently executed on multi-core processors. However, careful evaluation of the problem's suitability for parallelization and the potential overhead is crucial for optimal performance.

8.2 Libraries for Functional Parallelism in Python

Python, while not a purely functional language, offers several libraries that embrace functional programming concepts and can be leveraged for parallel processing. Here's a look at some popular options:

1. Multiprocessing:

Built-in library for spawning multiple processes and utilizing multiple cores.
Offers the Pool class for managing worker processes and distributing tasks.
Suitable for coarse-grained parallelism where tasks are relatively heavyweight (e.g., complex calculations).
Example:

Python
```
from multiprocessing import Pool

def square(x):
  return x * x


# Define data for parallel processing
numbers = range(10)


# Create a pool of worker processes
with Pool() as pool:
```

```
    # Use map to distribute the square function across
processes
  result = pool.map(square, numbers)

print(result)  # Output: [0, 1, 4, 9, 16, 25, 36, 49, 64, 81]
Use code with caution.
content_copy
```

2. Threading:

Another built-in library for creating and managing threads.

Useful for fine-grained parallelism where tasks are lightweight and I/O bound (e.g., network requests).

Requires proper synchronization mechanisms (like locks) to avoid race conditions when multiple threads access shared data.

Example:

Python
```
from threading import Thread

def download_file(url):
```

```python
    # Simulate downloading a file
    print(f"Downloading {url}")

# Define URLs to download
urls = ["url1", "url2", "url3"]

# Create threads for downloading
threads = []
for url in urls:
  thread = Thread(target=download_file, args=(url,))
  threads.append(thread)
  thread.start()

# Wait for all threads to finish
for thread in threads:
  thread.join()

print("All downloads finished.")
```
Use code with caution.
content_copy

3. Dask:

Powerful library for parallel computing in Python.

Offers task scheduling and execution across single-machine or distributed environments.

Provides abstractions for working with large datasets efficiently using parallel operations.

Example:

Python
```
import dask.array as da

# Create a Dask array (distributed array)
data = da.arange(10000)

# Apply operations in parallel across elements
squared = data * data
result = squared.compute()

print(result[:10])   # Output: The first 10 elements of the
squared array
```
Use code with caution.
content_copy

4. Joblib:

Offers parallel execution capabilities on multiple cores or distributed clusters.

Integrates with NumPy and SciPy for parallel scientific computing tasks.

Provides utilities for caching computations and memory management.

Example:

Python
```
from joblib import Parallel, delayed

def compute_something(x):
  # Simulate some computation
  return x * 2

# Define data for parallel processing
data = range(5)

# Run computations in parallel using Joblib
results                                        =
Parallel(n_jobs=2)(delayed(compute_something)(x)  for  x
in data)
```

```
print(results)  # Output: [0, 2, 4, 6, 8]
```
Use code with caution.

content_copy

Choosing the Right Library:

The choice depends on the nature of your parallelism problem.
Multiprocessing is good for coarse-grained CPU-bound tasks.
Threading is better for fine-grained I/O-bound tasks, but be cautious of race conditions.

Dask excels at parallel computations on large datasets.
Joblib simplifies parallel scientific computing tasks.

Remember: Consider the trade-offs between simplicity, performance gains, and potential overhead when selecting a library for your functional parallel processing needs in Python.

Chapter 9

Testing Functional Code

Testing functional code can be just as important as testing code written in imperative styles. Here's a breakdown of key considerations and approaches for testing functional code:

Focus on Functionality:

Functional programming emphasizes what the code should do rather than how it achieves it. Testing should reflect this focus.

Instead of testing implementation details, design tests that verify the function's behavior for various inputs and expected outputs.

Immutability and Purity:

Functional code is often immutable, meaning data structures are not modified during execution. This simplifies testing as the test doesn't need to worry about side effects affecting other parts of the code.

Pure functions (functions with no side effects and predictable outputs for given inputs) are easier to test in isolation. You can focus on input and output relationships without external dependencies.

Property-Based Testing:

This testing approach involves generating a large set of random test cases based on defined properties that the code should adhere to.

Libraries like QuickCheck (Haskell) or PropertySprouts (Python) can be used to automate property-based testing. These tests help ensure the code behaves as expected for a wide range of possible inputs, improving code robustness.

Example (Property-Based Testing in Haskell with QuickCheck):

Haskell
import QuickCheck

```
prop_doubleEvenPositive x = even (x * 2) ==> x >= 0
  where even x = x `mod` 2 == 0
```

```
quickCheck prop_doubleEvenPositive
```

Use code with caution.

content_copy

Exhaustive Testing:

In some cases, functional code might have a finite set of possible inputs. You can design tests to cover all these possible inputs and ensure the code behaves correctly for each one.

This approach can be particularly useful for small functions with well-defined input domains.

Matcher Libraries:

Many functional languages offer matcher libraries for testing purposes.

These libraries provide tools for conveniently comparing actual outputs with expected outputs, including handling different data structures and edge cases.

Example (Matcher Library in Scala with ScalaTest):

Scala

```
import org.scalatest._
```

```scala
object ListSpec extends FlatSpec with Matchers {

  "The map function" should "double all elements" in {
    val numbers = List(1, 2, 3)
    val doubledNumbers = numbers.map(_ * 2)
    doubledNumbers should equal (List(2, 4, 6))
  }
}
```

Use code with caution.

content_copy

Testing Frameworks:

Popular testing frameworks like unittest (Python) or Scalatest (Scala) can be adapted for testing functional code.

These frameworks offer functionalities like test setup, teardown, and assertions, which can be used to structure your functional tests effectively.

Remember:

There's no single "silver bullet" for testing functional code. The best approach depends on the specific codebase and its functionalities.

A combination of techniques like property-based testing, exhaustive testing, and matcher libraries can provide comprehensive coverage for your functional code.

By employing these testing strategies, you can ensure your functional code functions as intended, is robust, and easier to maintain in the long run.

9.1 Benefits of Testing Functional Code

Testing functional code, like any code, is crucial for ensuring it behaves as expected and delivers the desired results. However, functional programming offers some unique characteristics that make testing particularly beneficial:

Focus on Functionality:

Functional programming emphasizes what the code should do, not how it achieves it. Tests written for functional code should reflect this approach.

Instead of getting bogged down in implementation details, you design tests to verify the function's behavior for various inputs and their corresponding expected outputs. This focus on core functionalities ensures the code produces the right results regardless of internal implementation changes.

Immutability and Predictable Behavior:

Functional code is often immutable, meaning data structures are not modified during execution. This simplifies testing as the test doesn't need to worry about side effects from the code affecting other parts of the program.

Pure functions (functions with no side effects and a predictable output for a given set of inputs) are easier to test in isolation. You can focus on the relationship between inputs and outputs without external dependencies influencing the results. This focus on predictable behavior makes reasoning about the code's functionality much easier.

Early Detection of Errors:

By rigorously testing functional code, you can identify errors early in the development process. Functional programming's emphasis on immutability and well-defined functions often leads to smaller code blocks with clear responsibilities. This makes it easier to isolate and fix problems before they cascade into larger issues.

Improved Maintainability and Readability:

Well-written functional code tests act as documentation, explaining the expected behavior of the code for various inputs. This can improve the code's maintainability in the long run, as developers can understand what the code is supposed to do by reviewing the tests.

Tests can also serve as regression safeguards, ensuring that future code changes don't unintentionally break existing functionalities. As the code evolves, the tests act as a safety net to prevent regressions.

Examples of Testing Benefits:

Property-based testing: This approach involves generating a wide range of test cases based on properties the code should adhere to. It helps identify edge cases or unexpected behavior that might be missed with traditional testing methods.

Exhaustive testing: For functions with a limited set of possible inputs, exhaustive testing can ensure the code behaves correctly for all those inputs. This can provide a high degree of confidence in the code's functionality for specific use cases.

Conclusion:

Testing functional code offers a range of benefits that go beyond simply ensuring correctness. It promotes focus on core functionalities, improves maintainability, and fosters the development of well-reasoned and predictable code. By employing a combination of testing techniques like property-based testing, exhaustive testing, and matcher libraries, you can ensure your functional code delivers the expected results and remains robust in the face of future changes.

9.2 Techniques for Unit Testing Functional Programs

Functional programming offers a distinct style of development that benefits from specific unit testing techniques. Here's a breakdown of some key approaches to effectively unit test functional programs:

1. Property-Based Testing:

This technique focuses on verifying properties that the code should always uphold, regardless of specific inputs. Libraries like QuickCheck (Haskell) or Hypothesis (Python) can be used to generate a large set of random test cases that satisfy these properties.

Property-based testing helps identify edge cases and unexpected behavior that might be missed with traditional testing approaches.

Example (Property-Based Testing with Hypothesis in Python):

Python
```
from hypothesis import given, strategies as st

def double_even_positive(x):
  """Doubles an even positive number."""
  assert x % 2 == 0 and x > 0
  return x * 2


@given(st.evens(min_value=1))
def test_double_even_positive(x):
    assert double_even_positive(x) % 2 == 0   # Output should be even
  assert double_even_positive(x) > 0    # Output should be positive
```
Use code with caution.

content_copy

2. Exhaustive Testing:

Applicable for functions with a finite set of possible inputs.

You design tests to cover all these possible inputs and ensure the code behaves correctly for each one.

This approach can be particularly useful for small, well-defined functions.

Example (Exhaustive Testing in Haskell):

Haskell
```haskell
data Weekday = Monday | Tuesday | Wednesday | Thursday | Friday
  deriving (Show, Eq)

dayAfter :: Weekday -> Weekday
dayAfter Monday   = Tuesday
dayAfter Tuesday  = Wednesday
dayAfter Wednesday = Thursday
dayAfter Thursday = Friday
dayAfter Friday   = Monday

-- Test all possible inputs
```

```haskell
test_dayAfter :: Bool
test_dayAfter = dayAfter Monday    == Tuesday &&
        dayAfter Tuesday   == Wednesday &&
        dayAfter Wednesday == Thursday &&
        dayAfter Thursday  == Friday &&
        dayAfter Friday    == Monday
```
Use code with caution.

content_copy

3. Matcher Libraries:

Many functional languages provide libraries for conveniently comparing test outputs with expected outputs.

These libraries can handle different data structures (like lists, maps) and edge cases, making assertions more readable and maintainable.

Example (Matcher Library with ScalaTest):

Scala

```scala
import org.scalatest._

object ListSpec extends FlatSpec with Matchers {
```

```scala
"The map function" should "double all elements" in {
  val numbers = List(1, 2, 3)
  val doubledNumbers = numbers.map(_ * 2)
  doubledNumbers should equal (List(2, 4, 6))
 }
}
```

Use code with caution.

content_copy

4. Testing Pure Functions:

Functional programming emphasizes pure functions, which have no side effects and produce predictable outputs for given inputs.

Pure functions are easier to test in isolation as you only need to focus on the input-output relationship without worrying about external dependencies or mutations.

5. Mocking External Dependencies:

If your functional code interacts with external systems (databases, file systems), you might need to mock these dependencies during testing.

Mocking frameworks allow you to simulate the behavior of external systems in a controlled way, ensuring your code functions correctly even without the real dependencies.

Remember: The most suitable testing approach (or a combination of them) depends on the specific codebase and its functionalities. By effectively using these techniques, you can write comprehensive unit tests for your functional programs, leading to more reliable and maintainable code.

9.3 Property-Based Testing

Property-based testing is a powerful technique for testing software, particularly functional programs. It focuses on verifying properties that the code should always uphold, regardless of specific inputs. This approach offers several advantages over traditional testing methods:

Core Principles:

Shifting Focus: Instead of testing specific code paths or edge cases, property-based testing emphasizes ensuring the code adheres to certain general properties. These properties define the expected behavior of the code for a wide range of inputs.

Random Input Generation: Libraries like QuickCheck (Haskell) or Hypothesis (Python) are used to generate a large set of random test cases that satisfy pre-defined conditions. This helps uncover issues that might be missed by testing with a limited set of handcrafted inputs.

Shrinking Tests: When a property test fails, some frameworks can shrink the failing test case to a minimal failing example. This simplifies debugging by providing a smaller and more focused representation of the issue.

Benefits of Property-Based Testing:

Improved Coverage: By generating a vast number of random test cases, property-based testing explores a wider range of input scenarios compared to traditional testing. This can help identify edge cases and unexpected behavior that might be missed otherwise.

Focus on Functionality: The focus on properties encourages developers to think about the core functionalities of the code and how it should behave in general, leading to more robust and well-reasoned programs.

Early Error Detection: Random testing can expose errors early in the development cycle, before they become more difficult to fix.

Reduced Test Maintenance: Because property-based tests focus on general properties, they are less likely to become brittle as the code evolves. Changes that don't affect the core functionality won't break the tests.

Example (Property-Based Testing with Hypothesis in Python):

Python

```python
from hypothesis import given, strategies as st

def square_positive(x):
    """Squares a positive number and returns the result."""
    assert x > 0
    return x * x

@given(st.integers(min_value=1))
def test_square_positive(x):
    assert square_positive(x) > 0   # Output should be positive
```

Use code with caution.

content_copy

In this example, the square_positive function is expected to always return a positive value when given a positive input. The test uses Hypothesis to generate random integers greater than zero and verifies that the squared value remains positive.

Applications in Functional Programming:

Property-based testing aligns well with functional programming principles:

Immutability: Functional code often deals with immutable data structures. Property-based testing helps ensure that functions don't have unintended side effects and always produce the expected output for a given input.

Pure Functions: Functional programming emphasizes pure functions with no side effects. Property-based testing is well-suited for testing pure functions as you only need to focus on the relationship between inputs and outputs.

In conclusion, property-based testing is a valuable tool for unit testing functional programs. By focusing on properties and random test case generation, it helps developers write more robust, reliable, and maintainable code.

Part 4: Building Reliable Applications with Functional Programming

Chapter 10
Designing Clean and Maintainable Functional Applications

Functional programming offers a distinct approach to software development, and crafting clean and maintainable functional applications requires understanding these principles. Here's a breakdown of key concepts to consider:

Embrace Immutability:

Functional programming thrives on immutability, where data structures are created and remain unchanged throughout the program. This eliminates the need for complex synchronization mechanisms (like locks or mutexes) that can plague parallel programming in imperative styles.

By using immutable data structures, you simplify reasoning about your code's behavior. The state of the application is always clear, and you can easily track how data flows through your program.

Leverage Pure Functions:

Pure functions are the building blocks of functional programming. They take arguments, perform computations based solely on those arguments, and return a result without any side effects (like modifying global state or printing to the console).

Pure functions are highly testable and reusable as their behavior is predictable for a given set of inputs. You can easily compose pure functions to build more complex functionalities without worrying about unexpected interactions with external factors.

Focus on Declarative Style:

Functional programming encourages a declarative style, where you describe what the code needs to achieve rather than how it should achieve it step-by-step. This allows the compiler or runtime system to optimize and potentially parallelize the execution of your code.

By focusing on "what" needs to be done, you keep the code concise and readable. The underlying implementation details can be handled by the functional programming abstractions and libraries.

Utilize Higher-Order Functions:

Higher-order functions take functions as arguments or return functions as results. They are powerful tools for expressing complex logic and abstractions in a concise and reusable way.

Libraries like map, filter, reduce, and fold are common examples of higher-order functions that can be used to manipulate data collections and perform common operations in a functional style.

Prioritize Code Readability:

Functional code should be clear, concise, and easy to understand for both you and other developers. Use meaningful function names, proper indentation, and comments to explain complex logic.

Immutability and the use of pure functions contribute to readability as the code becomes less prone to unexpected side effects and easier to reason about.

Organize with Modules and Patterns:

Break down your codebase into well-defined modules that encapsulate specific functionalities. This promotes modularity and reusability.

Explore functional design patterns like the Command pattern or the Strategy pattern to structure your code for better maintainability and separation of concerns.

Testing is Essential:

Writing good unit tests is crucial for ensuring the correctness and reliability of your functional code. Property-based testing and matcher libraries are valuable tools in the functional testing toolbox.

Tests act as documentation, explaining the expected behavior of your code and improving its maintainability in the long run.

Additional Considerations:

Error Handling: While exceptions are generally discouraged, functional programming offers techniques like Maybe monads and Either types for representing optional values and handling errors more explicitly.
Performance: Not all functional code is inherently performant. Be mindful of potential performance bottlenecks and consider optimization techniques when necessary.

By adhering to these principles and embracing the core concepts of functional programming, you can design clean, maintainable, and well-structured functional applications that are not only efficient but also a joy to work with and reason about.

10.1 Functional Design Patterns

Functional programming, with its emphasis on immutability, pure functions, and higher-order functions, naturally lends itself to the use of design patterns that promote these concepts. Here's a breakdown of some common functional design patterns:

1. The Command Pattern:

Intent: Encapsulate a request as an object, thereby decoupling the sender of a request from its receiver. This allows for parameterization of clients with different requests, queuing or logging of requests, and undo/redo functionality.

Functional Umsetzung (Implementation):

Represent commands as functions that take the necessary data as arguments and return a new state or perform some side effect (potentially wrapped in a monad for error handling).
Use higher-order functions to store, queue, or execute commands.
Benefits: Improved modularity, loose coupling, and easier implementation of undo/redo functionality.

2. The Strategy Pattern:

Intent: Define a family of algorithms, encapsulate each one, and make them interchangeable. The strategy pattern lets you dynamically select which algorithm to use at runtime.

Functional Umsetzung:

Define different algorithms as separate functions.
Pass the desired function as an argument to another function, allowing for dynamic selection based on criteria.
Benefits: Promotes code reusability, reduces code duplication, and enables dynamic selection of algorithms.

3. The Observer Pattern (Pub/Sub):

Intent: Define a one-to-many dependency between objects so that when one object changes state, all its dependents are notified and updated automatically.

Functional Umsetzung:

Use callbacks or higher-order functions to define subscribers (functions) that will be notified of changes.

Implement a central pub/sub mechanism that maintains a registry of subscribers and triggers notifications when the state changes.

Benefits: Loose coupling between objects, simplifies dependency management, and promotes modular design.

4. Currying:

Intent: Transform a function that takes multiple arguments into a sequence of functions that each take a single argument.

Functional Umsetzung:

Higher-order functions can be used to create curried functions. By partially applying a function with some arguments, you create a new function that takes the remaining arguments.

Benefits: Improves code readability, allows for function composition, and can be useful for creating generic functions.

5. Partial Application:

Intent: Similar to currying, partial application involves fixing a subset of arguments for a function, creating a new function that takes the remaining arguments.

Functional Umsetzung:

Built-in language features or helper libraries can be used to achieve partial application.
Benefits: Promotes code reusability and can simplify function calls with many arguments.

Remember: These are just a few examples, and the functional world offers a vast landscape of design patterns. The key is to understand the core principles of functional programming and choose patterns that promote immutability, pure functions, and modularity in your code.

Sources

info

ckaestne.medium.com/thinking-like-a-software-architec
t-121ea6919871

10.2 Organizing Code for Readability and
Maintainability

In functional programming, clear and maintainable code
is paramount. Here are some key strategies to organize
your functional code for optimal readability and
maintainability:

Leveraging Functions:

Atomic Units: Break down your code into small, focused
functions that encapsulate specific tasks. This improves
readability and reusability, as functions act as
self-contained units of logic.
Meaningful Names: Use descriptive function names that
clearly convey the purpose of the function. This makes

the code easier to understand for both you and other developers.

Higher-Order Functions for Abstraction:

Abstraction Power: Utilize higher-order functions like map, filter, reduce, and fold to manipulate data collections and perform common operations in a concise and readable way. These functions abstract away boilerplate code, making your code more expressive and easier to follow.

Immutability and Pure Functions:

Clarity Through Immutability: Functional programming encourages immutability, where data structures are created and remain unchanged throughout the program. This eliminates the need for complex mutation logic, leading to cleaner and more predictable code.

Predictability with Pure Functions: Pure functions, a cornerstone of functional programming, take arguments and return outputs without side effects. This predictability makes reasoning about the code's behavior much easier and simplifies debugging.

Modular Design with Modules:

Modularization: Organize your codebase into well-defined modules that group related functions and data structures together. This promotes modularity, reusability, and separation of concerns. Each module should ideally have a single responsibility.
Clear Naming: Use descriptive names for modules that reflect their functionality. This improves code navigation and understanding of how different parts of your application interact.

Choosing the Right Naming Conventions:

Consistency is Key: Adhere to consistent naming conventions for functions, variables, and modules throughout your codebase. This improves readability and reduces cognitive load for developers working with the code.

Descriptive Names: Strive for names that clearly communicate the purpose of functions, variables, and modules. Avoid overly generic or cryptic names that leave developers guessing about their intent.

Effective Use of Comments:

Document Complex Logic: While functional code should be self-documenting due to its focus on what the code does rather than how, use comments to explain complex logic or non-obvious parts of your code.
Comments for Context: Comments can also be used to provide context, explain design decisions, or reference external resources for further details.
Code Formatting and Indentation:

Readability Through Formatting: Proper code formatting and indentation are essential for visual clarity. Consistent indentation helps developers understand the structure and nesting of your code.
Tools and Linters: Utilize code formatters and linters to enforce consistent formatting and identify potential

style issues. This ensures a clean and uniform codebase that is easier to read and maintain.

Testing is Crucial:

Confidence Through Testing: Write comprehensive unit tests to ensure the correctness and reliability of your functional code. This promotes code quality and makes it easier to identify and fix regressions when making changes.

Focus on Functionality: In functional testing, focus on verifying the expected behavior of functions for various inputs and their corresponding outputs, rather than getting bogged down in implementation details.

By following these strategies, you can organize your functional code for optimal readability and maintainability. This not only makes your code easier to understand and work with but also promotes long-term maintainability and reduces the risk of errors as your codebase evolves.

Chapter 11

Putting It All Together: Case Studies

Functional programming offers a unique approach to software development, often leading to concise, maintainable, and efficient code. Here, we'll delve into two case studies that showcase the benefits of functional programming in real-world scenarios:

1. Building a Simple E-commerce Application:

Imagine building a basic e-commerce application with functionalities like displaying products, adding items to a cart, and calculating the total price.

Immutability: We can represent products as immutable data structures with properties like name, price, and description. This simplifies reasoning about product data and avoids unintended modifications.

Pure Functions: Functions like addProduct or calculateTotal can be implemented as pure functions, taking a cart (data structure) and a product as arguments and returning a new cart with the added product or the total price, respectively.

Higher-Order Functions: We can leverage map to iterate through cart items and apply a discount function to each one. reduce can be used to calculate the total price by summing up the individual product prices.

Benefits:

Clean and Readable Code: The focus on immutability and pure functions leads to clear and concise code that is easy to understand and reason about.

Modularity: Functions encapsulate specific tasks, promoting modularity and reusability. Higher-order functions provide abstractions for common operations. Testing: Pure functions are easier to test in isolation, as their behavior depends solely on the provided inputs.
2. Developing a Data Processing Pipeline:

Consider building a data processing pipeline that reads data from a file, cleanses it, transforms it into a specific format, and then stores it in a database.

Immutability: We can represent data records as immutable data structures. Each processing step can create a new, transformed version of the data without modifying the original.

Pure Functions: Functions like cleanData or transformData can be pure functions, taking a data record as input and returning a new, cleaned or transformed record.

Function Composition: We can chain pure functions together using function composition to build the entire data processing pipeline. Each function operates on the output of the previous one, creating a readable and maintainable flow.

Benefits:

Parallel Processing: Functional code with pure functions can be readily parallelized for efficient processing of large datasets.

Error Handling: Functional programming offers techniques like Maybe monads to handle potential errors during data processing in a controlled manner.

Testability: Each stage of the pipeline can be tested independently using unit tests with pure functions.

These are just a few examples, and functional programming can be applied to various domains. The key takeaway is that by embracing core principles like immutability, pure functions, and higher-order functions, you can develop robust, maintainable, and well-structured applications that leverage the power of functional programming.

11.1 Building Real-World Applications with Functional Programming in Python

Python, while not a purely functional language, offers powerful features that enable you to leverage functional programming concepts when building real-world applications. Here's a breakdown of the key aspects to consider:

Functional Programming in Python:

Built-in Features: Python offers built-in features like first-class functions (functions can be assigned to variables, passed as arguments, and returned from other functions) and powerful iterators (like map, filter, and reduce) that support functional programming paradigms.

Libraries: Several libraries like functools (for higher-order functions) and itertools (for advanced iterators) provide additional tools for functional programming in Python.

Benefits of Functional Programming:

Immutability: Focus on immutable data structures (lists, tuples) minimizes side effects and leads to predictable program behavior.

Pure Functions: Functions with no side effects and predictable outputs for given inputs simplify reasoning about code and make testing easier.

Conciseness and Readability: Functional code can be more concise and readable due to its focus on what the code does rather than how.

Modularity: Breaking down code into smaller, reusable functions promotes modularity and improves code organization.

Potential for Parallelism: Functional code with pure functions can be readily parallelized for efficient processing, especially beneficial for data-intensive tasks. Challenges to Consider:

Performance: While functional code can be performant, certain patterns might require optimization compared to imperative approaches. Evaluate performance implications for your specific use case.

Debugging: Reasoning about complex logic built with chained function calls might require a different mindset compared to imperative programming.

Approaches for Building Functional Applications in Python:

Leverage Functional Libraries: Utilize libraries like functools and itertools to write concise and expressive functional code. Higher-order functions like map, filter, and reduce can be powerful tools for data manipulation.

Embrace Immutability: Whenever possible, represent data using immutable data structures. This simplifies reasoning about your code and avoids unintended modifications.

Write Pure Functions: Strive to write functions that take arguments and return outputs without causing side effects. This makes your code more predictable and easier to test.

Focus on Declarative Style: Describe what the code needs to achieve rather than dictating the step-by-step execution process. This allows for potential optimization and parallelization by the interpreter.

Organize with Modules and Patterns: Break down your codebase into well-defined modules with clear responsibilities. Explore functional design patterns like the Command pattern or the Strategy pattern for better code organization and maintainability.

Real-World Examples:

Data Analysis: Functional programming shines in data analysis tasks. Libraries like Pandas can be used with functional constructs to manipulate, transform, and analyze data sets in a concise and readable manner.

Web Development: Frameworks like Pyramid and Flask provide good support for functional programming principles. You can leverage functional approaches for handling user requests, processing data, and building web APIs.

Remember: Functional programming is a powerful tool in your Python development toolbox. By understanding its core principles and leveraging the available libraries, you can build clean, maintainable, and efficient real-world applications. However, it's crucial to evaluate the trade-offs between functional and imperative approaches to find the best solution for your specific needs.

11.2 Showcasing Benefits of Functional Techniques in Different Scenarios

here's a breakdown of how functional programming techniques offer benefits in various development scenarios:

Data Analysis and Manipulation:

Immutability: When working with data sets, functional programming's emphasis on immutability ensures clear data lineage. You can track transformations without unintended side effects, simplifying data analysis and debugging.

Pure Functions: Pure functions that process data without external modifications make it easier to reason about the transformations applied to your data. You can write functions focused on specific tasks, leading to cleaner and more predictable data pipelines.

Higher-Order Functions: Libraries like Pandas or tools like map, filter, and reduce provide powerful abstractions for data manipulation. You can process large datasets concisely and declaratively, focusing on what you want to achieve rather than low-level details.

Example:

Python
import pandas as pd

```python
data = pd.DataFrame({'name': ['Alice', 'Bob', 'Charlie'],
'age': [25, 30, 28]})
```

```python
# Filter adults with a pure function (no side effects)
def is_adult(row):
  return row['age'] >= 18
```

```python
adults = data.query(is_adult)   # Leverage function for filtering

# Map a discount function (pure) to each price
def apply_discount(price, discount):
  return price * (1 - discount)

discounted_prices = data['price'].apply(apply_discount, args=(0.1,)) # Apply discount with argument
```
Use code with caution.

content_copy

Web Development:

Immutability: In web applications, functional programming techniques can help manage application state. By using immutable data structures, you can represent the state of your UI components without unexpected mutations, leading to more predictable behavior.

Pure Functions: Pure functions that handle user interactions or data processing make it easier to reason about how your application reacts to user input. This can simplify debugging and testing of web components.

Declarative Style: Functional programming encourages a declarative approach, where you describe the desired UI state or data transformations. This allows web frameworks to handle the underlying logic, potentially enabling optimizations.

Example:

Python

```
# Simplified component function (React-like pseudocode)
def Counter(props):
 def handle_increment():
   return {'count': props['count'] + 1}  # Return new state object

  return {
    'count': props['count'],
    'on_increment': handle_increment
  }
```

Use code with caution.

content_copy

Concurrency and Parallelism:

Immutability and Pure Functions: Since functional code with immutable data structures and pure functions avoids side effects, it's inherently more thread-safe. This makes it well-suited for concurrent or parallel programming tasks where multiple threads might access the same data.

Declarative Style: The focus on what the code needs to achieve allows the runtime system to potentially parallelize the execution of your functional code, improving performance for CPU-bound tasks.

Example:

Python
```
from concurrent.futures import ProcessPoolExecutor

# Pure function to calculate factorials (no side effects)
def factorial(n):
  if n == 0:
   return 1
  else:
   return n * factorial(n-1)
```

```python
# Process factorials for multiple numbers in parallel
with ProcessPoolExecutor() as executor:
  results = executor.map(factorial, range(5))

  # Process the results (can be done concurrently as well)
  for result in results:
    print(result)
```
Use code with caution.

content_copy

These are just a few examples, and functional programming techniques can benefit various development domains. By embracing immutability, pure functions, and higher-order functions, you can write cleaner, more maintainable, and potentially performant code for various real-world applications.